BABUSHKA

poems by

Mary Avidano

Finishing Line Press
Georgetown, Kentucky

BABUSHKA

Copyright © 2018 by Mary Avidano
ISBN 978-1-63534-520-9 First Edition
All rights reserved under International and Pan-American Copyright Conventions.
No part of this book may be reproduced in any manner whatsoever without written permission from the publisher, except in the case of brief quotations embodied in critical articles and reviews.

ACKNOWLEDGMENTS

The author is grateful to the editors and publishers of poems included in this collection:

NEBRASKA LIFE published "To a Cottonwood Beside Lake Ericson, May/June, 2007; "His Book of Hours," November/December, 2007; "Orphan Train," January/February, 2008; "Before Spring" under the title "Late in the Winter," January/February, 2012; and "Escapade," September/October, 2015.
"Orphan Train" was included in TRAINS OF PROMISE, by Charlotte Endorf, Outskirts Press, 2011.
"To Those Young People at the Café" appeared in HIDDEN OAK POETRY JOURNAL November, 2007 in a similar version under the title "Letter to Young Readers."
"A Little-Known Book's Last Request" was published in HARP-STRINGS POETRY JOURNAL Autumn, 2009 under the title "A Little-Known Book Tells Its Dream."
"Chanticleer" won an honorable mention and was published in SILVER WINGS POETRY JOURNAL 2010 contest issue.

"Babushka" and "City Lights" were included in THE UNTIDY SEASON, an anthology published by The Backwaters Press, 2013.
"Fels-Naptha" appeared in 5 X 5 LITERARY JOURNAL June, 2014.
"City Lights" was featured in Ted Kooser's column, AMERICAN LIFE IN POETRY, December, 2014; also, in EVERYDAY POEMS, October, 2015.
Several of these poems were published in the author's earlier chapbook, THE ZEBRA'S FRIEND & OTHER POEMS, Zebra's Friend Press, 2008 and/or her blog at maryavidano.com.

Publisher: Leah Maines
Editor: Christen Kincaid
Cover Art: John Avidano
Author Photo: John Avidano
Cover Design: Elizabeth Maines McCleavy

Printed in the USA on acid-free paper.
Order online: www.finishinglinepress.com

Author inquiries and mail orders:
Finishing Line Press
P. O. Box 1626
Georgetown, Kentucky 40324
U. S. A.

Table of Contents

I.

Fireflies 1
Believer's Question 2
Keep a Green Tree in your Heart, And a Singing Bird
    Will Come 3
Message 4
Baggage 5
The Ink Still Bright upon Its Leaves 6
Gerard's Gift 7
To a Cottonwood beside Lake Ericson 8
Escapade 9
Street Lamp in Daytime 10

II.

It Was the Times 12
City Lights 13
I Ask Amiel 14
Orphan Train 15
Belonging 16
His Book of Hours 17
Fels-Naptha 18
Babushka 19
To the Sisters, Unsent 20
A Color of Blue 21

III.

Communion 24
The Preacher's Sunday Afternoon 25
A Little-Known Book's Last Request 26
Chanticleer 27
Northern Flicker at Work 28
Before Spring 29
In the Garden 30
Plum Thicket Haiku 31
To Those Young People at the Café 32
Return to Olson Nature Preserve 33

I.

Fireflies
> *We Friends believe the Light of God*
> *is in every person…*
> *—Philip Gulley*

These nights in June can they be seen
gliding to and from the little wood
where is hid my house.

Each bears aloft a light whereof
I do not know—except it says,
"Here I am, and here, and here."

Believer's Question

I know an agnostic
who has such radiance
as to cause one to ask
if God might not also
be found outside the fold.

**Keep a Green Tree in your Heart,
And a Singing Bird Will Come**
  —after a Chinese proverb

Today when we decided we'd go
look for some little scrub cedar,
I put on my raggedy coat. You
had on your frayed sweater and
anyway would wait in the car.

Did owl see us cross the pasture
or only the snowy sky?

Now tonight in our snug house
we breathe the fragrance of boughs
that once were adorned by garlands
of rain and of snow and starlight—
and, I am sure, by singing birds

returning when winters were past,
or droughts ended, or storms over.

Message

What I wrote once on a flat nondescript
pebble—*Whoever finds this, God loves
you*—was a confession of faith I left
that day on the riverbank. Perhaps it is
there yet, rinsed by dews of mornings,
dried in sunlight of days, until you in
the walking shoes should find it and
read and be heartened. If that is not to
be, then may this very stone be found
by a cricket with sand on its feet hoping
for a little warmth, as we all are when
night is coming on.

Baggage

The luggage rack atop the roof carries
her belongings of the life she is leaving.
She is not someone I know; I only happen
to see the car pass swiftly through town
just at sunset, its large luggage shadow
brushing the brick storefronts, windows
rolled down, her hair flying, radio music
streaming after. She is young, starting over.

I then get where I'm going, park under
the stately fragrant lindens, go down
the decrepit steps to the church basement.
One of the speakers this evening, a farmer,
the father of grown-up daughters and sons,
leans back in his folding chair, smiling
toward the ceiling or maybe to heaven,
his fingers laced behind his head. *You know,*
he says to us, *wherever you go, there you are.*

The Ink Still Bright upon Its Leaves

They all were anthologies,
the books of poems she bought
throughout the years, beginning
with The Pocket Book of Verse.

Its cover has gone missing,
pages falling out, brittle
and brown as the freckles she
has on the backs of her hands.

Today with the recklessness
of age she will buy a book
that has but one poet's work,
the poet's life written there.

Gerard's Gift
> *In 1868 Hopkins made a bonfire of his poems.*

At daybreak in a cold garden,
no friend there to keep me from it,
I tossed into the fire pages

torn from out of my old notebook:
dreams, loves, labors, every aspect
of myself I'd ever written.

I saw my words, their blackest ink,
on papers illuminated
the briefest time and turned to ash.

I might have been a butterfly
clinging to a branch, its wings wet
and quivering, as yet untried.

For seven long years I refrained
from writing poems, giving up
beauty to love my Maker more.

Then did God, not to be outdone,
bid me take pen in hand again
my remaining years—twice seven.

To a Cottonwood beside Lake Ericson

Ever a visitor of
ancient sanctuaries,
I step into the circle
of your befriending
shade, your leaves
tremulous to stillness
and to sighs like those
of grandmothers
who kneel alone
in houses of prayer.
When I go from here,
as reluctant as they,
I bring away
your whisperings.

Escapade

You know you live in a small town
when one bright morning in the fall
two horses galloping go by
your bedroom window, and you step
outdoors where they stop still under
the cottonwoods, looking at you,
breathing their freedom in crisp air
and in the same instant they bolt
away once more, huge and darkly
beautiful. You let the owners
know that Dolly and Kate are out,
and all day long you feel…chosen.

Street Lamp in Daytime

It stands in the public garden, beside
chrysanthemums and patterned paths
of brick. These five milk glass globes
are borne in so stately a manner upon
this slender fluted column of cast-iron

that I who love anachronisms begin
to suppose the gentlemen tip their hats
to ladies with parasols. We all are waiting
for dusk to fall over the garden and for
the humble lamplighter's touch of flame.

II.

It Was the Times
> *The gates will never be shut by day—*
> *and there will be no night there.*
> —*Revelation 21:25*

I.
There'd be a row of graves outside
the cemetery fence, unbaptized babies
or suicides or any others for any reason
not in the good graces of the church.

As for the fence adding sorrow
to sorrow, why did no one ever
take it down? As for the gates, why
were they not as it is in heaven?

II.

I know an old cemetery on a hill
where just outside the fence
can be found miniature iris
with flowers the deepest purple.

At first I took them to be exiles
banished from consecrated ground,
but no, they are the lilies of the field,
flourishing there in God's good graces.

City Lights
> *The lamplighter was finishing his rounds.*
> —Howard Hanke

My father, who was a quiet man,
told a story only the one time,
if even then—he had so little
need, it seemed, of being understood.
Intervals of years, his silences!
Late in his life he recalled for us
that when he was sixteen, his papa
entrusted to him a wagonload
of hogs, which he was to deliver
to the train depot, a half-day's ride
from home, over a hilly dirt road.
Lightly he held the reins, light his heart,
the old horses, as ever, willing.
In town at noon he heard the station-
master say the train had been delayed,
would not arrive until that evening.
The boy could only wait. At home they'd
wait for him and worry and would place
the kerosene lamp in the window.
Thus the day had turned to dusk before
he turned about the empty wagon,
took his weary horses through the cloud
of fireflies that was the little town.
In all his years he'd never seen those
lights—he thought of this, he said, until
he and his milk-white horses came down
the last moonlit hill to home, drawn as
from a distance toward a single flame.

I Ask Amiel
*To her great-grandfather on
4 October 1920, as it were*

Bricks you understand, their heft
and dimensions. All day long
you lay bricks, and there they stay.
At day's end, aching for rest,
you can stand and see your work
so lasting. Amiel, you love
even the color, sunset.

As to Anastasia's tears,
though, you are at a loss, and
as to a wayward daughter,
bewildered. Today you went
to work as usual—as you
had to, after all—knowing
Anastasia would obey.

You say she must take Annie
and the baby by streetcar
to the city, to the Board
of Public Charities—and
leave them. Therefore, Amiel,
I must ask you: this morning,
as you left, did you look in?

At that hour, with the children
all asleep—Frankie, Harold,
William, on their cots; and there,
Vera, Agnes, little Grace—
did you pause to bless this one,
your baby granddaughter, whom
you will never see again?

Orphan Train
> *Mother came to Nebraska*
> *on the Orphan Train in 1925*

Sister Michaela, named for an angel,
they followed you from the Foundling
home, their haven, to board the train
going west to prairies, to farms. Of all
the Sisters, you were best at this. You
knew how to keep the children quiet,
taught them to answer politely and to
show good deportment while standing
in a row on the wooden platforms, one
depot after another, one chance to be
chosen after another, the boys holding
their caps in their hands. In May, 1925,
Sister, you delivered a child to an older
couple who met the train at Omaha; the
mister said though they had hoped for
a boy—to help with the work—they'd
agree to take the girl instead. The four-
year-old with somber eyes and Buster-
Brown hair you had carefully combed
then, at your word, stepped forward
for the wife to take gently by the hand.

Belonging

In a box in which they'd kept
important things—farm receipts,
his Army medals—I find
a baby's bracelet. The three
initials engraved on it
in an ornate script
are mine.

His Book of Hours

When they fought over money,
we of the six worn-out out-
grown shoes tiptoed about the
falling-down ramshackle house,
heard Mother tell Father not
to bother coming home 'less
he'd gotten paid his wages.

Oh, but it was easier
to work hard all the long days
at this neighbor's farm or that
one's for a dollar an hour
except, of course in haying
season, when workers received
a dollar and a quarter—

easier for him than to
go back afterward to that
same good neighbor's front door and
stand around in useless talk
waiting for the man to say,
*Guess we should settle up—you
got your hours along?* Then forth
from Dad's left shirt pocket, the
one over his honest heart,
he brought his small notebook, its
exact penciled markings of
the days and hours, a living.

Fels-Naptha

Grandma, in taking cleanliness
for godliness, scrubbed whatever
needed it. *Never scrimp on soap,*
she'd say. Frugal Grandma, watching
her pennies, saved the rainwater
from off the roof to rinse her hair.

On wash day when the old rag rugs,
like our white underthings, were wrung,
our small hands reached up to fasten
the clothespins 'gainst the tugging wind.
Then we'd sit on the front porch step
near Grandma in her rocking chair.

Here in my sunny laundry room
I unfold the paper wrapping
from a brand-new bar of soap.
Breathing its fragrance is enough
to let me hear her say again,
First we do all our work, then rest.

Babushka
>*n. 1. A head scarf folded in a triangle and tied below the chin;*
>*2. in Russia and Poland, an old woman or grandmother.*

At fifteen I left my broken home
in Nebraska, entered a convent
in Chicago. This way at least I'd
always have a roof over my head,
the kindly grownups said with a sigh.
Once, at a bus stop on Pulaski,
a woman scolded me. Where is your
babushka? she wanted to know. So
I learned a new word that winter day.
Babushka—its syllables were as
satisfying as bread, caraway
rye the kitchen Sisters baked. "Is not
the body more than clothing?" asked our
Lord, seeing the lilies of the field.
Those first years, waiting to take the veil,
I little thought instead I'd marry,
give birth, become an old grandmother
feeding my chickens.

To the Sisters, Unsent

You saw that
I was only a child
in nun's clothing.
Even my prayers
were clumsy, often falling
through my fingers, getting lost.
I wanted to be like you.
I wanted to be like you,
clothed in comeliness, offering to God
the sweet fragrance of my kept vows.
O my sisters in Christ, I could not,
but look how faithful is God!
Prayers, tears are never lost,
nor do we fall through God's fingers.

A Color of Blue
For Raymond

It would be too much and too
sweeping a thing to say, that
blue is my favorite color—
like saying I love music
or poetry or am fond
of people. And so I will
note here only that blue is
sometimes the color of trees
and brush, on these smoky bright
afternoons in November;
diffused in light that touches
upon branches now shed of
their leaves—and this, that I am
and have been most fond of you.

III.

Communion

Worship was at eleven, now it is
past three, and I am at home again
on the porch, in my accustomed chair.

The porch screen, while keeping out
mosquitoes, gnats, and flies, lets in
all the great outdoors: breezes washing

through the cottonwoods, songs of birds
and of the first crickets, a neighbor's
wind chimes, the rumbling heartbeats of

youth cruising Main, three blocks over—
—and today, the first Sunday in August,
shimmering of poplars, silver cobwebby

threads adrift on nearer sky, shadows
of the blue spruce. I could wish to be
thus, neither a wall nor a window,

instead, an open soul, at peace; for as
was read in church today, God is above
all and through all and—think of this—in all.

The Preacher's Sunday Afternoon

We have been home barely only an hour
and he is thinking of his beloved garden
suffering in this hot wind again today.

From here I see a momentary hesitation
as he stands against the wind, his white
dress shirt and dark trousers billowing.

On his unsteady legs and with two canes
he starts down the little slope away from
the house. I wait to breathe 'til he is safely

settled in his chair beside the pepper plants
and in the orchard's shade, where he bends
to reach the hose left there from yesterday.

I think now I have a memory to keep, of how
the wind-tossed spray dampens those white
cuffs dried as soon again in the dappled light.

A Little-Known Book's Last Request

It is not as though I came from
the printers only yesterday.
I know very well what becomes
of us when we are old: with luck,
we end up dog-eared, smudged, cookie
crumbs lodged in our spines, coffee cup
rings upon our covers. For some
little time we're carried about,
insightful notations jotted
in our margins, parts of our text
underlined and some more than once,
until, of course, a newer book
comes along. Here at the thrift store
I hope for yet one more reader
although it ought to be enough
to be well thought of by a few.

Chanticleer

To attain an extra height he balances
on the threshold of the chicken run,
craggy toes splayed, while sounding
the announcement of a new day.

Here in the light of dawn he preens
plumage, cape and tail, his red comb
aglow and his male superiority still
among his most cherished delusions.

By the by, among the practical hens
scratching about in that little yard,
though a few say he's self-important,
to others he appears…magnificent.

Northern Flicker at Work

One would think fog muffles sound
instead of amplifying it; yet, this morning
in the dark my small world is gathered close.

Awakened by the sound of barking,
I've come outdoors. An echo is returning
bark for bark, Molly's unfortunate argument
with herself. Unclasping chain from collar
I watch her run ahead to our door, as though
just back from a far and dangerous journey.

In the sudden silence, in the fog,
it's then I hear from high in an unseen
tree, that miniature jackhammer.
Northern Flicker's workday
has begun. I am still in robe and slippers,
not even dressed, already late.

Before Spring

By afternoon of a day late in winter,
the snow has disappeared from the boughs
of the piney-wood hedge

and has left in its place large droplets,
all of them holding the sun. Here a dozen
sparrows flutter from one

low limb to the next, their slight weight
or brush of a wing sufficient to bless;
they send down as with hyssop
this welcomed prism'd rain.

In the Garden

Could you not wait one hour with me?
is a question others, too, may ask
in many a Gethsemane.

Plum Thicket Haiku

This road will take you
all the way to Easter's white
cloudbank of blossoms.

To Those Young People at the Café

My dears, if I may call you that:
at the care home where I will live
someday, others your age will be
calling me dear, wanting to know
am I going to finish my vegetables.

It's the years between our ages that
endears you, I suppose. Even now
I hope for one of you to look up
and return my smile as I slowly
button my coat and gather up my
scribbled poems. I must pass by your
crowded table on the way to the door.

Return to Olson Nature Preserve

Cross the footbridge, weary one,
enter the cottonwood grove
by the path you remember.

From there into the open,
a sandy trail leads northwest
and up to the highest ridge.

Follow dainty tracks of deer
southward, then, past the Burr oaks
and east, down to the Beaver.

No one calls it Beaver Creek,
only *the Beaver*, as though
it were a mighty river.

Here is where one day you saw
wild turkeys pass before you
with a rustling of dry leaves.

Wattles glowed red in late sun,
feathers gleamed as burnished bronze,
leaving a deepened silence.

Again from the bridge you say
every day would not be too
often, nor all day too long.

At the age of fifteen **Mary Avidano** left her childhood home, a farm in Nebraska, to enter a convent in Chicago. Twelve years later, she left the order to marry. She has a degree in English from Loyola University of Chicago and is an ordained minister in the United Church of Christ. Although she had written poetry occasionally all her adult life, it was not until 2004 that she saw her first poem published. That same year she received a grant to self-publish her first chapbook, THE ZEBRA'S FRIEND & OTHER POEMS (2008). BABUSHKA is her second poetry collection. Mary is the author of IN THE HOUSE OF I AM: A MEMOIR (2014) available through Amazon.com.

Mary lives at Elgin, Nebraska. Since her husband's passing in 2017, the love poems contained in this chapbook hold even more meaning to her.

www.ingramcontent.com/pod-product-compliance
Lightning Source LLC
LaVergne TN
LVHW041311080426
835510LV00009B/951